A PROJECT MANAGER'S HANDBOOK

A PROJECT MANAGER'S HANDBOOK

Graham Lashbrooke

KOGAN
PAGE

Copyright © Graham Lashbrooke 1991

First published in New Zealand in 1991 by L & A Publishers, 10 Silverstream Road, Crofton Downs, Wellington, New Zealand.

This edition first published in Great Britain in 1992 by Kogan Page Ltd, 120 Pentonville Road, London N1 9JN.

Reprinted 1994 and 1999

British Library Cataloguing in Publication Data

A CIP record for this book is available from the British Library.

ISBN 0-7494-0759-X

Typeset by BookEns Ltd, Baldock, Herts.
Printed and bound in Great Britain by Clays Ltd, St Ives plc.

Contents

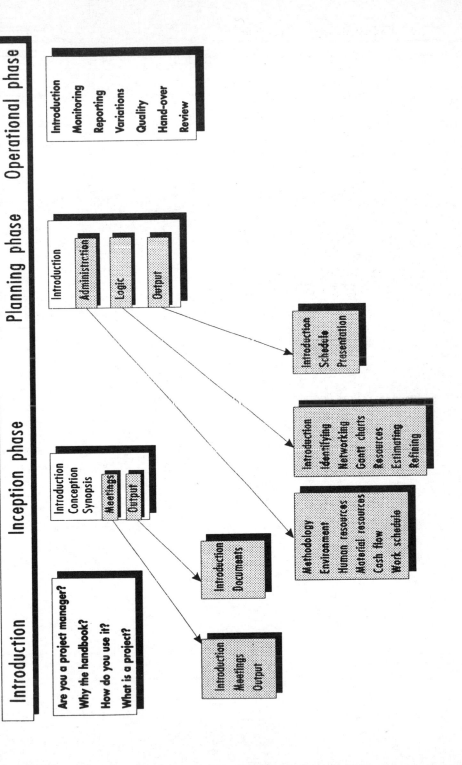

Introduction | Inception phase | Planning phase | Operational phase

Introduction
- Are you a project manager?
- Why the handbook?
- How do you use it?
- What is a project?

Inception phase
- Introduction
- Conception
- Synopsis
  - Meetings
  - Output

- Introduction
- Meetings
- Output

- Introduction
- Documents

- Methodology
- Environment
- Human resources
- Material resources
- Cash flow
- Work schedule

Planning phase
- Introduction
  - Administration
  - Logic
  - Output

- Introduction
- Identifying
- Networking
- Gantt charts
- Resources
- Estimating
- Refining

- Introduction
- Schedule
- Presentation

Operational phase
- Introduction
- Monitoring
- Reporting
- Variations
- Quality
- Hand-over
- Review

1. Introduction

> **The most successful project managers are those who take painstaking trouble to understand all aspects of the projects they control, plan their strategy meticulously, and follow through by carefully monitoring and controlling the operational phase. Above all, successful project managers are deadly serious about their responsibilities and are always examining their work critically.**

Are you a project manager?

The project manager has a central role, vital to the success of the project:

1. You are *the great communicator* for, not only must your project team know exactly what they have to do, but all the people concerned about the success of the project must know as well.

2. Becoming the manager of a project, whether it is by tender, choice or order, means you are contractually responsible for the success of the project.

3. It is your duty to ensure that the contract you enter into is attainable and that, if it is not, you inform the project owner before you start and either agree changes to the project limitations or refuse to carry it out if no agreement can be reached.

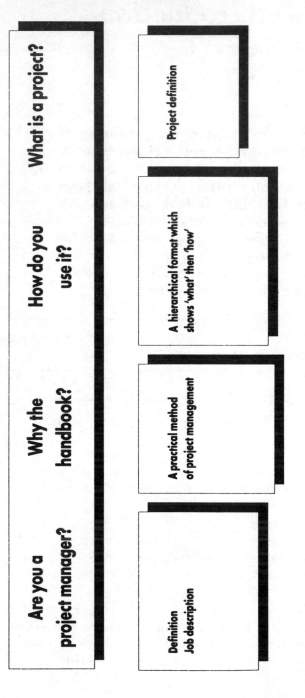

Are you a project manager?

Definition
Job description

Why the handbook?

A practical method of project management

How do you use it?

A hierarchical format which shows 'what' then 'how'

What is a project?

Project definition

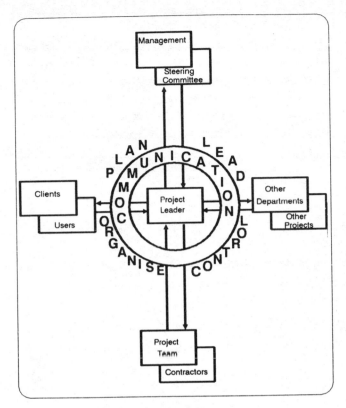

Figure 1.1 *The great communicator*

4. If a project which you are managing fails, you are the person who must carry the responsibility and explain the reason for that failure.

The responsibilities are onerous. This handbook will show you how to avoid the many pitfalls by working through a project step by step. It is a handbook for people who *really* want to be effective, practical project managers.

A little later, the inception phase of the project will discuss specific ways in which organisations can be structured to ensure that you can fit into the traditional company hierarchy and *still* have the necessary authority and accountability for the project.

The project manager is the person who is accountable for the successful completion of the project. The project manager plans, leads, organises and controls the project and ensures that communication links are clearly established and used.

Why the handbook?

It is important for you to know the rationale behind the development of the handbook.

Although much has been written about project management, I realised there was nothing available in a practical handbook format, and therefore set about writing this book.

The purpose of the handbook, therefore, is to provide you with a practical working method for managing projects, all in one volume. You need never look further than this book when managing future projects and, if you are not an experienced project manager, you can attend a training course which will teach you how to manage projects effectively according to its principles.

Furthermore, knowing that users of the handbook will have varying levels of experience, I have structured it so that you can easily access only those parts which you need.

Although you will be able to use the principles presented as a standard in your organisation, I am not giving you a project management methodology. The reason for making this comment is that I am not presenting a bold new approach to project management – there isn't one – I am simply stating in a clear, structured way an approach which has been used successfully over a wide range of disciplines for many years.

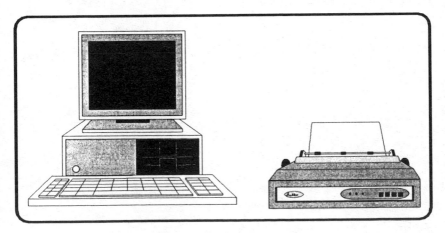

Figure 1.2 *Computer (left) and printer*

It follows, therefore, that, if you are using a computerised project scheduling package (and I sincerely hope you are) it can comfortably be used to carry out the techniques described.

Throughout the handbook I shall recommend the use of computerised project scheduling packages because I believe that you will manage your projects more successfully if you use one. However, the handbook is not a reference guide to the selection of a specific package; it is up to you to carry out that investigation within your organisation. What I can say is that all the popular packages are suitable, with strengths and weaknesses in different areas.

Throughout they will be referred to as computerised project *scheduling* packages because I do not want you to fall into the trap of using them actually to *manage* your projects. Remember that *you* manage the project; the computer simply assists with documentation to enable you to maintain your schedule.

How do you use the handbook?

It is important to understand the format of the handbook so you are able to use it effectively:

1. It is written for **you**, the project manager, personally. It therefore uses the pronouns 'you' and 'yours' throughout and I refer to myself using the personal pronoun 'I'. As you read the handbook, imagine you are on a practical project management course being addressed by the tutor.

2. It is formatted in a highly structured way to provide easy access, to take you through the development of a project over the three phases which I have called the inception phase, the planning phase and the operational phase. Each phase is introduced by a short overview.

3. The project phases are presented with a number of activity headings, each new heading appearing on a new page.

4. I have taken into account varying levels of project management experience when describing project management activities, and have therefore presented them in the following format:

The guide

This is a series of hierarchical diagrams which precede phases and sections of the handbook and which effectively map and summarise the sections they precede. The diagrams show all the headings, most of which are followed by a short explanatory description to answer the question: 'What must be done?' If you are an experienced project manager or you know *how* to do the specified activity, you need read no further than the guide.

The method

This follows its hierarchical diagram. It is a longer, more detailed explanation which answers the question: 'How must it be done?' The answer to this question is often supported by answers to additional questions which ask 'why', 'who', 'where' and 'when'.

In designing the handbook, I have taken great care with the format. I believe this has resulted in all sections of the method being easy to access. I have also incorporated many explanatory diagrams to back up the text where necessary.

5. You can confidently use the principles described in the handbook; they have been tried and tested by experienced project managers and have been declared practical.

I ask you to consider the structured format of the handbook for therein lies the secret of effective practical project management. Structure your project documents similarly by using diagrams to introduce and summarise the sections.

Remember that a well-presented diagram is worth a thousand words.

What is a project?

A project can be defined as a group of related activities with a beginning, a middle and an end.

It is divided into three definite phases called the inception, the plan and the operation.

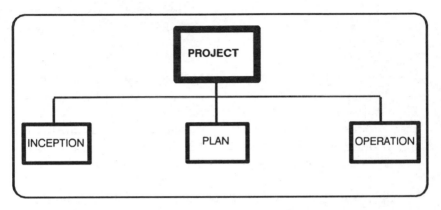

Figure 1.3 *Three phases of a project*

It has an objective which can be quantified by three main factors: time, money and quality.

It can be considered successful when the project owner, who is the person at the top of the project reporting chain and on whom the ultimate responsibility for decision-making rests, is satisfied with the quality and completeness of the output and it has met its time and budget constraints.

It can be considered partially successful when the project owner is satisfied with the output in spite of time or budget over-runs.

It is a failure if the project owner is not satisfied with the output, or the time and budget over-runs.

Dennis Lock, who has written a number of excellent books on project management, summarises projects within four different categories:

Civil engineering, construction, petrochemical and mining, which are the kinds of project that first spring to mind whenever project management is discussed. They are probably also the projects that are most successfully managed. Generally, the operational phase is completed at a remote site from the contractor's office, and such projects are usually exposed to the elements which, apart from the inherent risk, introduce special problems associated with organisation and communication. Because they generally have a huge budget, they require intensive management of progress, cash flow and quality of output.

Manufacturing projects which are geared to producing a piece of machinery, a ship, an aircraft, a car, or computer hardware. They are usually conducted in a factory and are often geared to mass production of their output. Often the installation of the end product is carried out on the customer's premises and involves training the customer's staff.

Management projects which are usually a result of a management decision to move premises, develop and install a new computer system, prepare for a major marketing function, or any other activity that involves management of activities resulting in a measurable output. Interestingly, more and more companies are changing their approach to line management by saying that most line functions can be given a deadline, a budget, and a measurable output and, as a result, be declared a project.

Research projects which usually take a long time, consume vast amounts of money and have an end result which may be disappointing. Those termed fundamental research are often started to see if it is actually possible to produce a stated end product and can therefore be considered successful if, after a reasonable length of time, it proves to be either possible or impossible. The expenditure on these projects is difficult to control and the cut-off time almost impossible to assess.

The rest of the handbook is going to take you on a guided tour through a project. Use the principles described and, like many before you, you will find that the method works, it is practical, and it will make you a better project manager.

Introduction   Inception phase   Planning phase   Operational phase

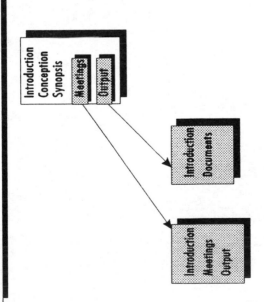

2. The Inception Phase

Introduction

As a project manager, your role during this phase of the project's development is to ensure that the contract you are entering into is both practical and feasible. Although the project owner will be in control, this in no way minimises the importance of your role, for you must provide advice during meetings, correct misunderstandings, be the communications link between technical and non-technical members of the project management board, and above all find out as much about the project as you can.

Remember that it is your responsibility to draw up the contract at the end of this phase and, if you are not in full possession of the facts, the contract is incomplete and the project is likely to fail.

Before describing the activities of the inception phase, we shall define the people involved.

The project sponsor

The project sponsor is a person or a group of people responsible for financing the project.

The project owner

The project owner is a person appointed by the project sponsor who forms the first link in the reporting chain, who reports directly to the project sponsor, and carries the responsibility for all major project decisions.

The project management board

The project management board, which I shall refer to as the PMB, is a group of people chaired by the project owner and comprising the project sponsor(s) and selected representatives

Introduction · Conception · The project synopsis · The conceptual meetings · The output

Introduction

Definitions for:

Project sponsor
Project owner
Project management board
The contractor
Project manager
Sub-contractors

Conception

The reason why the project owner needs the project

The project synopsis

Drawn up by the owner, containing:

The reasons
The output
Any known constraints
A suitable contractor

The conceptual meetings

Introduction
Organisation structures
Handling meetings
Output from the meetings

The output documents

Introduction
Output documents

of both. You report to this body and always attend their project development meetings.

The contractor

The contractor is the company employed by the PMB which is contracted to carry out the requirements of the project.

The project manager

The project manager is a person appointed by the contractor to manage the project.

Sub-contractors

Sub-contractors are appointed by the project manager through the contracting company and generally with the approval of the PMB.

In a small in-house project, the owner may also be the sponsor and the project management board all rolled into one and simply referred to as the customer. The contractor, who would most likely also be the project manager, would be an employee of the company who has been put in charge of the project.

The staff of the company who report to the project manager and who carry out the project activities could be considered the sub-contractors. Typical of this would be a small computer project to improve the company's accounts receivable system which employs the accountant as the project manager, a systems analyst as the main sub-contractor, and programmers as the junior sub-contractors.

At the other end of the scale in a very large project, there may be many people involved in the management of the project in every capacity and the contractor could be appointed from a group of companies that tendered for the job. Sub-contractors who are specialists in providing the different output requirements would be appointed by the project manager. Typical of this would be a high rise development in the centre of town which would be controlled by a contracting company, managed by one or more of their own project managers, and use a number of sub-contractors at various times during the operational phase of the project.

I shall use an 'improved accounts receivable system' and a 'large high rise development' throughout the handbook as examples to back up explanations.

The point to be made here is that it does not really matter about the size of the project, the hierarchical disciplines remain the same, moving only from simple to extremely complex.

Throughout the handbook I shall refer to the names defined in this section and ask that you apply them according to the nature of the project. I also ask that you do not play down responsibilities of the project members simply because the project may be small.

Conception

Projects are conceived for a number of reasons. These include:

- The sale of a specific project to a client
- A change within the client company
- The advent of new technology
- A change in the political environment
- A desire to remain competitive
- Entry into a profitable venture
- An existing entity requires alteration.

Whatever the reason or reasons, the customer makes it known that a project has been conceived as a result of the perceived reason.

Unless you gave the customer the idea for the project in the first place, you are not likely to be involved at this point.

The customer who requested the project may become the project owner or an owner could be appointed by the customer, in which case the customer then becomes the project sponsor.

The project synopsis

The project owner draws up a synopsis of the project to identify:

The reasons for the project

This identifies what motivated the customer to consider the project. It is important to know this reason, however trivial, because it answers the question: 'Why are we doing this project?'

The required output

The customer draws up an outline of the project requirements which could consist of sketches, narrative, or a combination of both which identifies as much as is known at this stage.

In an improved accounts receivable system this may consist of the format of some new reports, a short explanation of the content and two or three meetings for clarification, while in a high rise development this would include plans, rough sketches, references to previous developments, a full description, and meetings to clarify all the complex issues involved.

Any known constraints

The three major constraints on any project are time, money and quality. At this point it may be impossible to assess any of them accurately but it is important that rough estimates be given by the customer to assist you in the development of the plan.

A suitable contractor

An organisation or a single person must be contracted to develop the project.

In the case of an improved accounts receivable system this would simply be an order from the accountant for an available and suitable systems analyst to be the main sub-contractor, while in a high rise development it would be the successful contractor chosen from a number of companies which tendered for the job. The successful contractor would then appoint a suitable project manager from within their ranks or from a specialist project management organisation.

Because of the many unknowns, the *synopsis* will contain vague statements and probably many suggestions. It will more than likely change as more facts become known during initial meetings and again later during the planning phase as the project detail becomes apparent. However, this is a very important document because it contains the first conceptual thoughts of the project owner, and because it becomes the basis for discussion during the conceptual project meetings.

Introduction   Organisational   Handling meetings   Output from the meetings
structures

The point at which you join the project

Project team organisation

Matrix organisation

Find out everything you can about the project

Ask questions – find out: 'what', 'why', 'when', 'how', 'where' and 'who'

Confront all difficult issues

Clarify all points, even small ones

Deliverables – the output and quality

Project limitations – money and time

Necessary conditions for success (NCS) – quantified objectives and purpose

Project policy – identifies top level reporting lines, your responsibilities and scope of authority; conflict resolution method, cash flow during planning and operational phases, and sources of human and material resources

The conceptual meetings

Introduction

At the first conceptual meeting of the PMB, a decision will be made to progress further or to abandon the project at this stage. If the decision to proceed is taken, a project manager is appointed. This can simply be an in-house selection of a suitable person, or the result of a successful tender. In either case:

> **This is the point at which you join the project.**

Organisational structures

As promised in the introduction, it is important to discuss company hierarchical structures that enable a project manager to work across departmental boundaries within an organisation and, at the same time, be given the necessary authority. In short, everyone must be aware that a project is under way. The reasons I stress this point are:

- There is a need to override the ongoing power struggles and political manoeuvres that are constantly happening within an organisation.
- Everyone must be aware of their role, however minor, in the successful completion of the project.
- Project management is relatively new to many organisations and would benefit from publicity.
- Projects are often taking place at the forefront of an organisation's strategic plans and can therefore be seen as vital to the continued success of the organisation.

There are two basic ways in which an organisation can be structured in order to ensure that projects are managed successfully. These are:

A project team organisation, in which the project manager is given responsibility and accountability for all aspects of the project as well as the clear authority of direct command. An organisation which adopts this policy has obviously realised the importance of well-controlled projects. The results of a project team structure are:

- Maximum authority for the project manager
- No ambiguous lines of command
- Good staff motivation because of the simple and clearly understood management structure
- An ability to run and control large projects using a high percentage of the available staff.

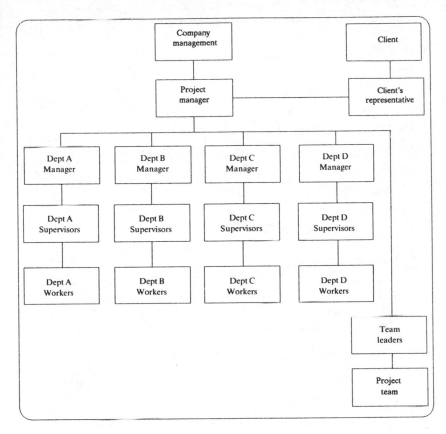

Figure 2.1 *Project team organisation*

A matrix organisation, in which project managers are allocated teams from different departments within the organisation. The team members report in the normal way to their own line managers but have a reporting link to their project manager as well. The results of a matrix structure are:

- Flexible deployment of the organisation's resources
- Effective availability of experts
- An ability to run many small projects at the same time
- Good staff motivation because of career paths into specialist areas.

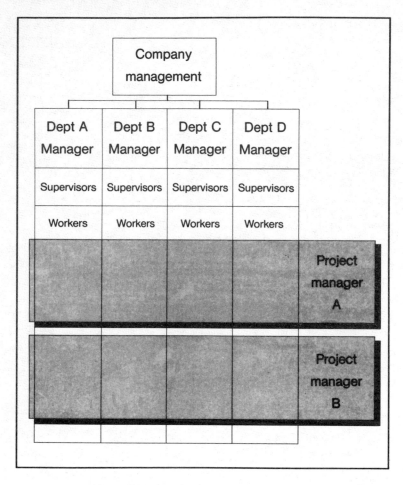

Figure 2.2 *Matrix organisation*

We have now reached the point where a series of meetings of the PMB at which you are present take place to discuss the project, and ultimately to decide whether to proceed or to abandon it.

The nature of these meetings and how to handle them are described on the following pages.

Handling meetings

A series of meetings of the PMB at which you are present take place to discuss the project, and ultimately to decide whether to proceed or to abandon it.

Before I discuss what must be decided at the meetings, a word or two about your conduct during them.

Remember your role is to find out everything you can about the project. Never waver from that objective.

You find things out by asking questions. People will only volunteer what they consciously remember; questions will jog their sub-conscious. Learn this verse by heart:

I keep six honest serving men
(They taught me all I knew);
Their names are what and why and when
    And how and where and who.

Repeat it to yourself during meetings to remind you to ask questions. You ask the questions identified in Rudyard Kipling's poem to discover:

- **What** the project is going to achieve – the objectives.
- **Why** the project was conceived – the reason the customer thought of it in the first place.
- **When** the end results are required – the time scale.
- **How** the work is to be done – the quality of the output.
- **Where** the project is to take place – the environment.
- **Who** is going to do the work – the sub-contractors or the project team members.

You may only be a junior member of the PMB, but do not make this an excuse to avoid confronting difficult issues.

If you fail to clarify a relatively small point at this early stage, it is likely to develop into a much more difficult obstacle later.

Output from the meetings

The conceptual meetings identify the following:

The deliverables

This is the answer to the question, 'What is required in terms of both output and quality?' Do not allow any deliverable to be vaguely stated because it is likely to lead to a project which produces a different output from the one desired.

The project limitations

This identifies the limitations on money and time and therefore on people and materials. Because these are high level discussions, everyone is aware that there could be minor changes later, but this does not mean that the limitations should not be treated seriously.

One of the apparent anomalies of the project development life cycle is that a limitation on time and money is stated *before* any detailed planning is done. However, when one considers that most projects have some form of precedence and therefore a basis for calculation, it is not such an anomaly. Besides it is important to you to know the limitations within which you must plan the project so that you are not tempted to present a Rolls-Royce solution to a Mini Minor problem or vice versa.

In the rare case of a project which has no known precedence, the time and money limitations are more likely to be inaccurate and, as a result, you will more than likely be asked to present your estimate of time and cost *after* the planning phase.

Remember that it is extremely rare for a project to be so unique that no person can be found, and no documentation can be researched that can provide a basis for calculating the limitations.

Necessary conditions for success (NCS)

This is the name I have given to the overall quantified objectives and purpose of the project. Having identified the deliverables and the limitations placed on them, by coupling these with the project purpose, you arrive at the necessary conditions for success. It is a known fact that the reason many projects fail is because the necessary conditions for success were never clearly identified or were wrongly identified during the conceptual stage of the project.

Although you are the project manager, in a large project you may only be controlling sub-contractors who report to you and who, in their turn, have a project team that carries out the specific section of the project that requires their unique expertise. It follows, therefore, that you need only specify the high level necessary conditions for success to the sub-contractors reporting to you, and they in turn will develop them for their teams. I mention this to introduce the concept of the hierarchical structure of a project, a method of breakdown that I strongly recommend.

The project policy

This is an important administrative part of the conceptual meetings, and is to ensure that all parties are aware of how this project is to be controlled. Normal project management standards, if you have them in place, will cover most administrative aspects. I list below the factors which must be clarified:

Top level reporting lines

This is to ensure that there is no confusion later about who should have told who something, or who didn't report something correctly.

Responsibilities of the project manager

It is not sufficient simply to say you are in control of the project. You must clearly spell out exactly what your role is, to whom you directly report, and how you will get the necessary finance, among other items.

Authority of the project manager

Because a project is a one-off operation which may exist within established line management roles, it is vital at this stage that you know the exact scope of your responsibility. I have already discussed two ways in which an organisation can be structured to allow you to exercise the necessary authority. I suggest you re-read these. You can find them under the heading 'Organisational Structures' on page 32.

Method of conflict resolution

In line with the previous point, it is vital to know at this stage who will mediate in cases of conflict. Projects are often held up or stopped completely by conflict, the solution for which was not clearly spelled out before the project started.

Cash flow during the planning and operational phases

There is nothing more embarrassing than having to plead for money as it carries with it all the connotations of begging. How much better to have a policy for financing the project clearly spelled out before the project starts. This policy should also include finance for unexpected situations. In the case of a small in-house project where the financing may simply be an inter-departmental financial transfer, this should still be treated as seriously as a multi-million pound budget project. Interdepartmental transfers are often referred to as 'funny money'. I suggest that this should be changed to 'serious money' to help ensure that the right attitude is maintained by all who are employed on the project.

Sources of human and material resources

In the case of small in-house projects these factors are known because they will consist of your staff and the materials known to be available in the organisation. However, in larger projects which employ many sub-contractors for specialist activities, they are very much more difficult to co-ordinate. Just as the project owner developed a list of suitable contractors, you should have a similar list of specialist and available sub-contractors.

Introduction

Where the project contract
is drawn up and signed

Output documents

Project map of functions – a hierarchical diagram of the
functional relationship of all project members: PMB at the top
followed by project manager, then sub-contractors

Project map of necessary conditions for success – also
hierarchical but shows objectives and purpose at each level of
the hierarchy

Project proposal – a binding contract between you and the PMB
as well as binding contracts between you and sub-contractors
and between sub-contractors at each hierarchical level

The output

Introduction

We now arrive at the output stage of the conceptual phase. Up to this point the conceptual meetings have been gathering more and more information and clarifying all the known details of the project. It is time that this is clearly formatted. Clarification is necessary to show how you intend tackling the project, remembering that you still have only a high-level concept of the requirements. You must also produce a proposal which clearly spells out the terms of your contract with the project owner.

Output documents

I have adopted the policy that a diagram is worth a thousand words. We have examined the major requirements of a project proposal and have distilled most of the output into two diagrams called project maps.

Mapping is a way of hierarchically depicting the major structures of the project. I have used a hierarchical diagram because everyone is familiar with them and they are easily understood. The two project maps describe the functions and the necessary conditions for success. Let us look at the nature of these documents:

A project map of functions

This is a hierarchical diagram which presents a high-level picture of the functional relationship of all the project members. It therefore clearly defines personnel responsibilities, their reporting lines and their involvement in the project. It is partly a result of the project policy decisions made earlier in that it shows reporting lines, your responsibilities and the role of sub-contractors.

If your organisation is arranged in either the project team or matrix structures described earlier, you will have very little trouble producing this diagram. If, however, your organisation treats every project as a one-off, you will have to draw a diagram to fit the current personnel arrangements. This in itself is good motivation to consider creating permanent project management structures.

For in-house or one-off projects the PMB is placed at the top of the hierarchy and you are shown under it and reporting directly to it. After that the number of hierarchical levels will depend on the number of departments involved in the development. The effect of this map is that everyone concerned is absolutely clear about their role and hierarchical importance.

If you work for a construction company the business of your organisation is running projects. There will already be clear reporting lines defined so all you have to do is put names against the personnel who are to be involved. Then, because you will probably have to employ sub-contractors to handle specialist areas, you will add them to the map, with names where possible,

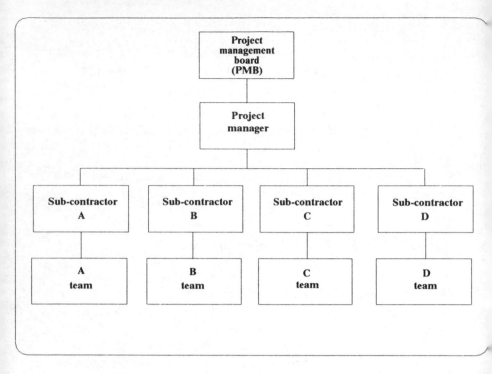

Figure 2.3   *Function project map*

and clearly show their reporting lines either directly to you or indirectly through one of the other project members.

Whether illustrating a small in-house project or a large one being developed by a contracting company, the diagram must be supported by a number of documents, including:

- Your contract with the PMB
- The contracts between you and the sub-contractors
- Details of who the sub-contractors are, why they were chosen and maybe their track records.

From this point on I shall refer to this diagram as the functional project map.

A project map of necessary conditions for success

This is related to the functional project map in that the format is similar but, instead of identifying the personnel involved, it shows the objectives and purpose at each level of the hierarchy. It is in effect a diagram of the project deliverables, and the limitations.

At the highest level of the hierarchy the necessary conditions for success will be the deliverables and the limitations for the entire project, while at lower levels they will apply for that section of the project only. In this way the objectives, quality of output and time constraints become totally clear to each project member for, at the lowest level of the hierarchy, they become the necessary conditions for success for individual tasks.

This project map remains an important document during the planning and operational phases of the project. It provides a link between the conceptual and the later phases and is reproduced in greater detail as more factors about the project become known.

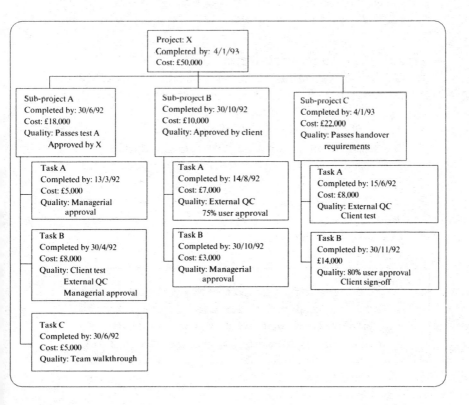

Figure 2.4   *Project map of necessary conditions for success (NCS project map)*

From this point on I shall refer to this diagram as the NCS project map.

The project proposal

The final output from the conceptual phase is a project proposal. It is your responsibility to draw this document up and it is a distillation of all that has been learned at the conceptual meetings and from independent research.

As a result of this proposal a binding contract is drawn up between you and the PMB. It does not matter whether the project is a small in-house one or a large one conducted by a specialist project management organisation; it is absolutely vital that this binding document is drawn up. If there is no such document, there is no contract for you to carry out the project and no come back from either side if the project fails. It is obvious that this would be a totally untenable situation and must be avoided at all costs.

The contractual document

To summarise, the output from the conceptual phase of a project is the contract document which contains the following:

- An introductory overview of the project
- NCS project maps with supporting documents
- Functional project maps with supporting documents
- A summary of the costs at each stage with final totals
- A summary of the time scale for each stage and an overall time
- The project proposal.

You now have a project contract which has been agreed to and signed by all parties and you are fully prepared to enter the planning phase of the project.

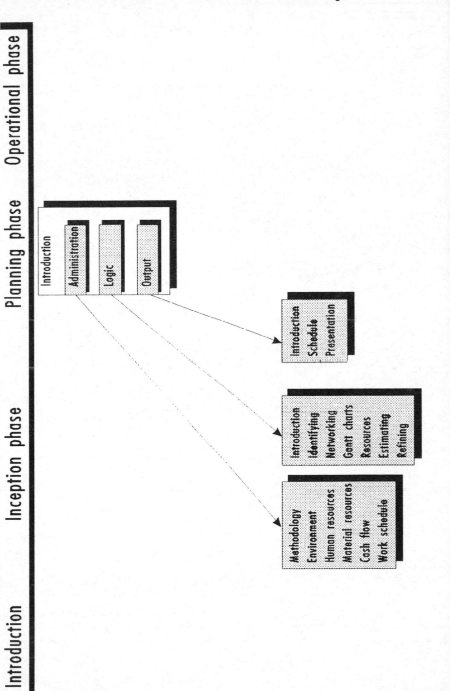

3. *The Planning Phase*

Introduction

The project contract is signed. At the conceptual level you have a clear understanding of all you must do in order to complete the project successfully.

As you enter the planning phase, do so with this in mind:

> **More projects fail through insufficient or bad planning than all the other reasons combined.**

From this point on the project is under your control and, while you still have a definite reporting link to the PMB, you must make the many decisions that will go towards ensuring that the project is a success.

During the planning phase you must:

- Finalise detailed administrative procedures
- Develop and document a logical breakdown of the project plan
- Produce a document called the project schedule which provides the contractual link between the planning and operational phases.

Introduction

- More projects fail through insufficient or bad planning than all the other reasons put together

Project administration

- Project management methodology
- Project environment
- Human resources
- Material resources
- Cash flow
- Daily work schedules

Logic definition

- Introduction
- Identifying the activities
- Networking the activities
- Gantt charts
- Allocation of resources
- Time estimates
- Refining the model

Planning output

- Introduction
- The project schedule
- The presentation

Project administration

Introduction

During the conceptual phase you helped to define the project administration policy. This established your role, how you were to resolve conflicts, the cash flow, and where your human and material resources originated.

These must now be further refined. The following pages describe the steps required to refine the administration policy.

Project management methodology	Project environment	Human resources	Material resources	Cash flow	Daily work schedules
Adopt the method of the handbook to your own organisational standards	Understand and, if necessary, survey the project environment	Sub-contractors are already identified on the functional project map	Identify and ensure supply of general materials which are your responsibility	More detailed breakdown at sub-contractor level	Your daily schedule includes:
		All project members are managers of their own section no matter how insignificant	Ensure sub-contractors have their own material requirements		Planning – on your own for the project future
					Meetings – with PMB and sub-contractors
					Reporting – to keep adequate flow of communication up and down
					Leading, organising and controlling – to provide leadership and direction

Project management methodology

No doubt you and your organisation have a set of standards which are brought into effect during the management of all projects. I have already addressed this a number of times in the conceptual phase. If you do not have a standard approach, I suggest you adopt one immediately.

> **Planning and operational standards are always to be found at the heart of a successful project.**

If you do not have project management standards, the time to develop some is right now. I have said that the handbook does not promote a methodology but rather describes an effective method for managing projects. Therefore I suggest you adopt the following process in order to develop your own methodology.

Use the methods described in the handbook and make sure that everyone involved in the project development has a copy.

Incorporate a hierarchical organisation chart and identify people outside the project who are responsible for such things as finance (the accountant), materials (the purchasing officer), resources (the human resources manager), training (the training manager), and so on.

Investigate and decide on a computerised project scheduling package.

As a guide:

- Ask suppliers for the brand names of the most popular packages that can work in a networked environment.
- Make a short-list of about three.
- Get advice from a consultant.
- Make sure that everyone in the organisation who is going to be involved in this and any future projects knows which package has been selected. Show and explain the reporting facilities offered so that they know not only what progress reports will look like, but also how to interpret them.

You now have all the basics of a methodology. It's so painless it makes you wonder why organisations take so long to develop and adopt standards!

As I have raised the subject of computerised project scheduling packages, this is a good time to discuss them. First, and most important, remember that they are *scheduling* not *management* tools. *You* are the manager and you are using the package to help you plan and keep control of the project schedule. Management is all about communicating with other people, while a scheduling tool will help to provide the hard copy output; it will not be able to influence, guide, counsel and discipline the project members like you can.

Having said all that, I unreservedly recommend that you make use of a scheduling tool, not only for the standardisation of your reporting, but because a computer has the value of being able to hold information so that it can be changed, retrieved and accessed for enquiry extremely easily.

Project environment

Know the environment in which you are going to control the project.

In the case of an in-house improved accounts receivable computer system, this is simply where the team and the materials, such as computer terminals to be used in the development of the project, are sited.

In a high rise building development, which would be built on a site geographically separate from your organisation, it could involve survey maps, local environmental conditions and geological samples before the environment can be declared suitable, and then the materials required will have to be transported to the site, probably a portable site office.

Human resources

The functional project map has already identified the project team or, in the case of a multi-level hierarchical map, sub-contractors reporting to you. It follows that, if there is more than one level in the hierarchical reporting line, those sub-contractors will have project teams or further sub-contractors reporting to them.

Let us examine the hierarchy of functions further in order to be certain of the responsibilities and authority of all project members. It is already apparent from the previous paragraph that sub-contractors, although they report to you, the project manager, would, in their own section of the project, be considered project managers by their own team. It follows, therefore, that the definition of a project manager in the first section of the introduction applies equally to sub-contractors.

This process can be taken right down to the lowest level of the hierarchy where, in the case of an improved accounts receivable system, you would find the programmers and, in a high rise development, the artisans and labourers. Each of these people at the lowest level doing perhaps single tasks, such as writing programs or laying bricks, is in fact the project manager of those tasks. The definition in the introduction applies equally well to those with no management responsibilities identified at the lowest level of the functional project map. It is important that the handbook is read by the entire team and not just those involved in managing the project!

> **Everyone who forms part of a project development team is in effect a project manager.**

Therefore it does not matter if someone's role in a project is to complete only one activity. This activity becomes a project in their eyes and is subject to all the disciplines of project manager. For instance, they must be totally aware of what they have to do and the time and cost constraints in force. This is a good time for you to refer to the first introductory section of the handbook, 'Are you a project manager?' Remember that, as part of your professional leadership, you must motivate your whole team to treat their tasks, however minor, with the same professionalism. I repeat the definition of your role here:

> **The project manager is the person who is accountable for the successful completion of the project. The project manager plans, leads, organises and controls the project, and ensures that communication links are clearly established and used.**

To avoid confusion I will not refer to everyone concerned with the project as a project manager, but will continue to use the terms sub-contractor and project team.

Material resources

All projects need material resources to aid their completion. In the case of an improved accounts receivable system these may consist of only stationery and computer terminals; a high rise development requires many specialised materials such as portable offices, cranes, trucks, and the tools of the various sub-contractors involved. Apart from these requirements, there are the standard materials always available in every office such as desks, chairs and other furniture.

This may also be a good point to mention your computerised project scheduling package. It should simply be treated as one of the material resources. In the case of larger projects which make use of sub-contractors it is desirable, but not always possible, to ensure that all project members are using a similar package to standardise the reports.

Most organisations involved in major project work develop excellent relationships with their favoured sub-contractors. If this is the case in your organisation, extend that relationship by suggesting that they standardise on the same package as the one you are using.

Cash flow

The overall flow of cash to finance the project was established during the conceptual phase. However, each sub-contractor must be aware of their individual cash flows, so a more detailed breakdown is required.

You, through the PMB, have overall responsibility for the supply of money into the project, but each sub-contractor must identify their own needs to you in order to ensure a smooth and adequate flow of finance into each hierarchical level of the project. Many large projects have come to a temporary and costly stand-still simply because the cash was not made available at the required time.

Whether you are managing an in-house project where the financing consists of interdepartmental transfers or a large project requiring a huge capital outlay, you should have a clearly developed, budgeted plan.

Daily work schedules

I have made it apparent that you must have extraordinary organisational powers to ensure that the project runs smoothly and successfully. So far I have defined your role as one of organising other people. But what of the organisation of your own time and input to the project?

Let us look at the work schedule of a typical day in the life of a project manager.

Planning

During a project there is always a need for planning, even during the operational phase. Many macro plans developed at this stage must be re-examined during the operational phase to produce detailed micro plans. This is a time when you need to be on your own, a difficult thing to achieve if you are the central cog in the project wheel. The only way to do this effectively is to set aside a specific time every day which is to be your private time, and to make sure that project members are aware of it.

Meetings

You may consider meetings a bore or a necessary evil. I believe that meetings, if handled well, are the most effective means of ensuring that all concerned are kept aware of progress, problems and changes, and provide a forum for instant decision-making. I do not suggest daily meetings with the PMB or your team; this would be an excellent way of ensuring that nothing gets done while everyone has a great time talking about it. I do suggest, however, that the PMB and your team are kept regularly informed through meetings. Rather than take the easy way out and simply set aside Monday morning for meetings, call them when the need arises. Here are some suggestions to ensure that you conduct meetings efficiently:

- Treat each meeting as a mini-project with all the discipline that entails.
- Make sure that you have a clear objective and purpose for calling a meeting.

- Send out an agenda before the meeting to allow everyone time to prepare.
- Put your own privately estimated times against agenda items to enable you to control the discussions.
- If you are chairing the meeting make sure that you are in control of the time, subject matter and the attendees. Be assertive and make sure that everybody is aware that *your* meetings run to time, stick to the point and avoid unnecessary conflict.
- Start the meeting at the advertised time whether everyone is there or not. If someone arrives late and as a result misses discussion on a point they wanted to address, do not reintroduce the item but explain that arriving on time will in future ensure that they can address all items. If this happens a couple of times you will soon find that people arrive at *your* meetings on time!
- If a discussion is running on too long ask the central parties to call a separate meeting to discuss and resolve this issue and report their decisions or recommendations at the next meeting.
- Have someone take minutes at the meeting and insist that these are typed and presented to the attendees within one day after the meeting.

Reporting

If a report conveys the message adequately, do not make it the subject of a meeting.

Use reports at meetings to avoid long discussions. Distribute them early and then simply ask for agreement or comments at the meeting.

Most organisations have reporting standards. You must know these and use them. If you are using a computerised project scheduling package, you have an excellent built-in progress reporting mechanism. However, as I have suggested earlier, make sure that everyone understands how to interpret the output.

Leading, organising, controlling and co-ordinating

The most necessary part of the day is exercising your leadership role, yet it is the one area most often neglected. The reason for this is that it is the most difficult, for leadership involves resolving conflicts, allocating leave, rescheduling tasks, disciplining, counselling, appraising, and countless other confrontational tasks.

If you have any doubt in your mind about your ability to handle confrontation, I strongly suggest you insist on training in this area. As a start towards improving your leadership techniques, I offer these suggestions:

Practise effective listening
This may almost have become a cliché, but I ask you to treat it very seriously. Becoming a good listener requires learning some techniques followed by constant practice. These include:

- Unblock your ears and your mind
- Avoid distractions
- Use eye contact
- Use encouraging door openers
- Ask lots of open questions
- Summarise for clarity
- Reflect your understanding of the meaning
- Feel the speaker's emotion
- If applicable, record salient points.

Become more assertive
Assertive people are those who control their own lives; their destinies are not controlled by others. Think how many times the situation has arisen in your life when you have said to yourself, 'I wish I'd spoken up at the time – now it's too late.' Timing is all-important in becoming more assertive. If you let a situation pass you by you minimise and, in some cases, totally negate, the impact when you do finally speak up. Like listening, assertiveness requires that you learn some techniques followed by constant practice. These include:

- Become a good listener
- Speak your mind clearly and at the right time
- Conquer the fear of saying no

- Suppress assertiveness-sapping emotions such as anxiety, paranoia and guilt
- Refuse to treat people differently for gender or racial reasons
- Be persistent when stating what you want
- Enter into negotiation and come to a clear compromise
- Use an even voice tone and maintain eye contact
- Do not use minimising words such as 'sort of'.

Understand yourself
So many people disadvantage themselves by not understanding their own strengths and weaknesses. I suggest that, if you are one of them, you rectify the situation immediately, possibly by taking a training course.

Whatever method you use, you will find that once you understand your own strengths and weaknesses, you will be better equipped to build on your strengths and to work on minimising your weaknesses.

Practise an adjustable leadership style
A continuum of leadership styles has the authoritarian at one end and the democrat at the other. An authoritarian leader brooks no interference in decision-making; subordinates are told what to do and are severely reprimanded when they do not carry out instructions to the letter. The democrat, on the other hand, allows complete freedom within the policy laid down by the organisation; subordinates manage their own jobs and only refer to the manager to get more or to hand in completed work.

From the above you may infer that the best leadership style to adopt would be somewhere between the two extremes. This is not true. You must be able to adjust your leadership style depending on the maturity and behaviour of the subordinate you are dealing with.

For instance, if you have just employed someone with little experience who is going to learn the job by getting practical experience, a little bit of the authoritarian is called for to ensure that work is done properly to your parameters. If, however, you have someone in your team who is very experienced and responsible, playing the democrat is not out of place. The point here is that you adjust your leadership style to suit the situation.

Introduction

Identify how the project is going to be done

There are no short cuts to proper planning

Identifying the activities

Use the NCS project map as a base

Lower level sub-objectives become individual activities

List activities with standard times if known

Networking the activities

The purpose is to:

Sequence the activities

Identify logical groupings

Identify parallel groupings

Identify activities on the critical path

Identify non-critical activities

Drawing guidelines:

Insert milestones at ends of groups

One start and one end node

Avoid danglers

Avoid looping

Draw in a single direction

Identify critical monitoring points:

Expected overtime

Critical completion dates

Material arrival dates

Inspection points

Gantt charts

Use as a communication tool

Some information as a network diagram, plus:

Shows delayed activities

Shows overlapping activities

Shows float time

Useful for resource allocation

Allocation of resources

Requirements:

Time estimates

Lead times

Cost estimates

Percentage of time used

To reduce overall time:

Use more experienced human resources

Increase human resources

Upgrade material resources

Downgrade the quality

Phase the project completion

Use histograms to:

Identify over-allocations

Show availability

Show collective resource usage

Level resources

Report

Time estimates

Absolutely must be done accurately

Guidelines:

Get personal experience

Use experience of others

Use documented experience

Document your own experience in a standards manual

Make use of an estimating technique

Refining the model

Planning is an iterative process

Repeat:

Identifying activities

Networking activities

Developing Gantt charts

Allocating resources

Estimating times

And carry on until results are correct and acceptable

Logic definition

Introduction

At the end of the conceptual phase we were able to draw up two project maps.

First, let us look at the NCS project map.

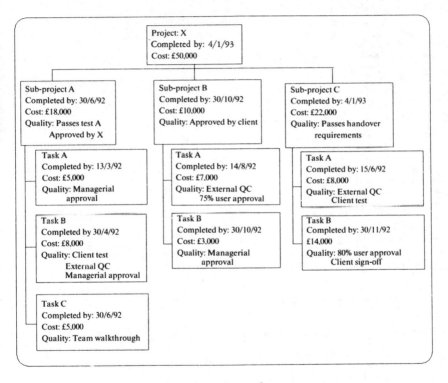

Figure 3.1 *Necessary conditions for success project map*

At each hierarchical level of this map you are able to identify:

- **Why** the project or this hierarchical level of the project was conceived
- **What** objectives must be achieved for successful completion
- **When** the overall project and each stage must be completed.

The other map was the functional project map, also hierarchical, which identified all the people involved in the project from the members of the PMB to the lowest level sub-contractor.

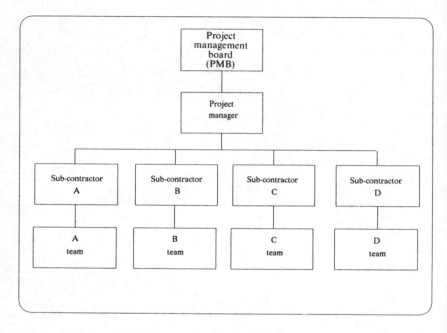

Figure 3.2 *Function project map*

From this map you are able to identify:

- **Who** is going to achieve the necessary conditions for success identified in the NCS project map.

By ensuring that the administration details were all taken care of at the beginning of the planning phase, you were able to identify:

- **Where** the project is to take place.

At the end of the conceptual phase you established, at a high level, how you were going to achieve the project goals. Now is the time to revisit that conceptual plan and refine it in more definite terms. What you now have to do is establish:

- **How** the project is to be achieved.

Remember that, because our approach to the management of the project has been hierarchical, there are a number of people, the sub-contractors, who each have to produce a plan showing how they intend to achieve their part of the project. This has the effect of reducing the overall size of the project by breaking it up into a number of manageable chunks. However, the hierarchical approach means that each plan, although developed independently, is inexorably linked by the overall and individual time scales, and therefore dependent on the plans of other project members. It is your role as project manager at the highest level of the hierarchy to collate all plans, ensure that there are no anomalies, and finally produce an overall plan that represents the entire project.

This may sound like a difficult, if not impossible, task but in reality it is quite easy. This is because you do not have to know the detail of each plan, you need only know what it is to achieve and when, and this information is already available from the NCS project map. Of course, when the sub-contractors do their detailed planning, some of the time scales may change. This is acceptable within the overall constraints of the project and must be entered on the NCS project map to ensure that it remains an up-to-date document.

If you are using a project scheduling package, collating the various plans into an overall one is even simpler because most of the better packages operate hierarchically. This becomes even easier if you have agreed with all project members that they use the same package.

Now it is time to look at the techniques you will use to plan your project. They have been used for many years by successful project managers and include network diagrams, Gantt charts, resource allocation and estimating. If this prompts you to think, 'Oh, what a pity, I thought I was about to learn a new magic formula for developing a plan!', take refuge in the knowledge that it is better to use a method that has wide acceptance and usage than one which no one is likely to understand. Also be aware that planning is an exact task requiring total commitment in which every 'i' must be dotted and every 't' crossed if it is to be effective.

> **There are no short cuts to proper planning.**

Although the techniques are described roughly in the sequence in which they are carried out, remember that you will often have to cycle back and forth through each of them in random sequence as new facts become known. This is known as refining the plan and is a very important part of the whole process.

I have presented a project as a hierarchical structure. I have shown how each sub-project run by each sub-contractor is a project in its own right which, when added to all the other sub-projects, makes up the entire project. We are now about to discuss the production of the project plan under the broad heading of logic definition. However, to simplify our explanation and therefore your learning process, we will ignore the hierarchical nature of a project and simply talk about a single level controlled by you, the project manager, with a PMB to whom you report and a team waiting to carry out your plan. You in your turn must realise that our description would work equally well for a small sub-project within the main one.

> **Stop here! Are you using a computerised project scheduling package? If so, good, because now is the time to use it.**

Identifying the activities

At the lowest hierarchical level of the NCS project map, the objectives for carrying out specific sections of the project are defined. If these objectives are broken down further they become the specific activities required to achieve the objectives.

This is the real power of the NCS project map. It ensures that no matter how far from the overall project objective you are, you are always in harmony with the rest of the project.

So your first step towards developing the plan for your project is to identify the activities. This may sound difficult but it is usually very simple, for it can be assumed that you are managing a project within your field of expertise. Hence:

- A civil engineer will manage bridge building projects
- A structural engineer will manage high rise buildings
- A software engineer will manage a computer system development
- A craftsman will build a dining room suite
- An electrician will install the wiring for a house
- A plumber will install a bathroom.

In all these disciplines there are standard activities, some of which will have to be adapted slightly to cater for the unique specifications of the prevailing project.

At this stage you simply make a list of the activities required to carry out the project. Do not worry about the sequence or the time scales, they will come later. Of course, in most cases, the sequence will be correct because of the logical progression of your thoughts and because many are standard activities anyway. You will also have no trouble allocating time scales to some of the standard activities either. While I recommend that you record as much as possible, do not hold yourself up just because you are unaware of some minor details.

Most organisations which use computerised project scheduling packages have developed project management guidelines which list all the possible activities with standard times where applicable. This list is imported into the package and used to create the unique list for the prevailing project. This is done by removing activities which do not apply and adding some unique ones. This method has the advantage of:

- Drawing up a comprehensive and probably correct list of project activities very quickly
- Acting as a jog to the memory
- Providing you with most of the standard timings for activities
- Creating an organisational standard approach to project planning.

Networking the activities

Introduction

Network diagrams were developed in the 1950s as a method of modelling projects and have been in use in various forms ever since.

There are two main types of network diagram known as *Activity on arrow* (AOA) and *Activity on node* (AON). The first to be developed was the AOA method which is known as Critical Path Analysis (CPA) or Performance Evaluation and Review Technique (PERT). The AON method, simply called a network diagram, has a more formal method of presentation and is the one used by most computerised project scheduling packages. Because I have advocated the use of computer scheduling tools, I shall refer to the AON method in our description of network diagramming. However, to ensure that you are aware of and understand both methods, they are both described below:

Activity on arrow (AOA). In this method the arrows represent activities and therefore occupy time, and the nodes, which are drawn as circles, represent an event and therefore a point in time.

Figure 3.1 shows part of Figure 3.2 as an activity on arrow network diagram. Note the following:

- The activities and their times are shown on the arrows
- The circular nodes are events, i.e. points in time
- The node at the start of an activity is called the tail event and that at the head, the head event
- When naming activities the identities of the tail and head events are referred to, therefore activity Turn Legs is called T10/T11.

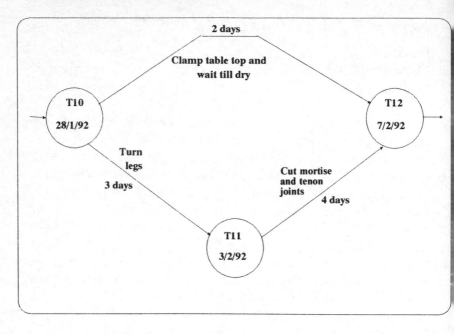

Figure 3.1 *Activity on arrow network diagram (AOA)*

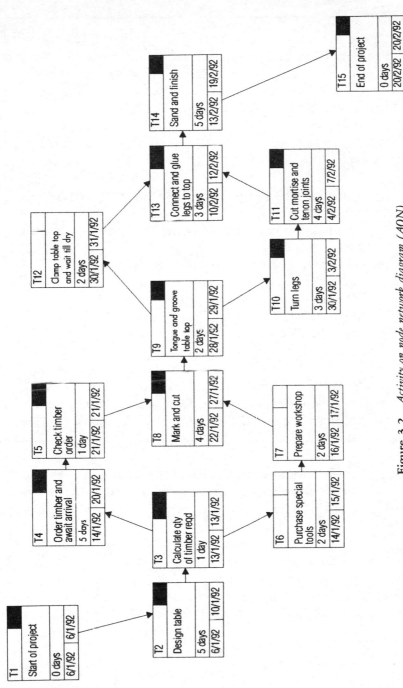

Figure 3.2 *Activity on node network diagram (AON)*

Figure 3.2 shows a network diagram using the activity on node (AON) method of drawing. This is a one-person project to build a wooden table with lathe-turned legs, probably in the carpenter's home workshop. Note the following points which will all be addressed in the text:

- The identity number in the top left-hand corner of each node (T1 . . . T15)
- The black rectangle in the top right-hand corner of each node indicating critical activities and therefore the critical path
- The description of the activities in the centre of each node
- The elapsed time in days just below the centre. The time scale for this project is in days, therefore this becomes the minimum time even though some activities take less than 1 day.
- The start date in the bottom left. Note that weekends have been excluded.
- The end date in the bottom right, which is the start date plus the elapsed days. Weekends are excluded.
- The milestone nodes at the start and end of the project which are identified by having zero elapsed days.

Essentially the technique is to build up the activities in the project using a series of arrows connected to nodes which can be either boxes or circles. Connecting the project activities in this way identifies:

- The linear sequence of the activities
- Groups of activities which can occur in parallel
- The time scale for logical groups of activities
- The overall time scale for the project, which is known as the critical path
- Project milestones or stages
- Float time

- The estimated end time in a forward scheduling project and the required start time in a reverse scheduling project.

Typical conventions are:

- The diagram is drawn from left to right, the arrow heads showing direction.
- Each activity has an event at either end, the one at the start being the tail event and the one at the head, the head event.
- An event can be simply an insignificant junction between two activities; it can represent a milestone or stage, or it can be the start or end event of the project.
- The events are numbered in sequence from left to right always ensuring that, in the case of an event common to two groups of activities, the head event is numbered higher than the tail.

Activity on node (AON). In this method the arrows are merely connections between the nodes, drawn as rectangular boxes which represent activities and events at the same time.
   Typical conventions are:

- The diagram is drawn from left to right or from top to bottom with minimal crossing lines.
- Apart from an identity number, the activity nodes contain the start, elapsed, end and float times.
- Activities with a zero elapsed time are inserted throughout the diagram to represent milestones or stages. These are in effect events rather than activities because they happen at a point in time.
- The first and last nodes always have a zero elapsed time.
- The critical path is identified by highlighting the activities along it.

The activity on node network diagram in Figure 3.2 shows all these conventions.

Definitions

Before dealing with the practical issue of building your project model using a network diagram, let us define some of the terms used in network diagramming:

Predecessor is an activity or event that immediately precedes the one currently being processed (see Figure 3.3).

Successor is the activity or event that immediately succeeds the one currently being processed (see Figure 3.3).

Float time is the difference between the necessary time for an activity or group of activities and the time available (see Figure 3.4).

Early free float or free float is the float which is possessed by an activity which, if used, will not change the float in later activities (see Figure 3.4).

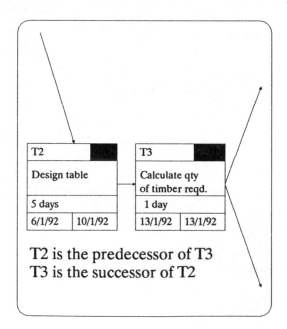

T2		T3	
Design table		Calculate qty of timber reqd.	
5 days		1 day	
6/1/92	10/1/92	13/1/92	13/1/92

T2 is the predecessor of T3
T3 is the successor of T2

Figure 3.3   *Network diagram forms 'predecessor' and 'successor'*

Independent float is the float possessed by an activity which, if used, will not change the float in any other activity (see Figure 3.4).

Critical path is that sequence of activities which determines the total time for a project (refer to Figure 3.2 which shows the critical path).

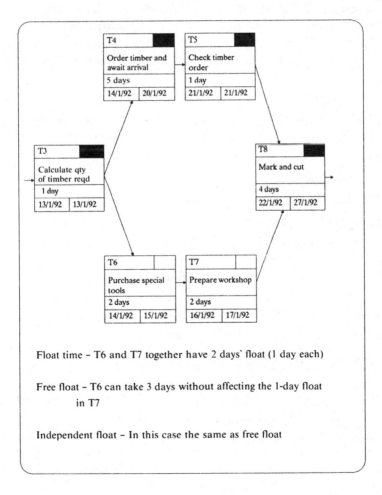

Float time – T6 and T7 together have 2 days' float (1 day each)

Free float – T6 can take 3 days without affecting the 1-day float in T7

Independent float – In this case the same as free float

Figure 3.4 *Float times*

A dangle is an activity whose completion does not give rise to either another activity or the completion of the whole project.

A loop is an illogical sequence of activities in which a later activity is shown linked back to an earlier one.

The process

You must first sequence the list of activities in logical groups and then arrange the groups in parallel, where they can be carried out at the same time, and serially, where they can only occur sequentially. Parallel groups of activities should start and end at a common node referred to as a milestone node.

At this point you can enter the following information in each node:

The identity

This may simply be a number or any other unique way of referring to it. A computerised scheduling tool will provide an automatic incremental identity number for each node.

A description

This tells in a few words what the activity does.

Estimated elapsed time

If you know the time scale enter it.

Later, as the network becomes more complete you add the rest of the time scales, after which you are in a better position to add more information to the nodes. Before doing this, however, you must be aware of whether you are using reverse or forward planning. *Reverse planning* is knowing the end date of the project and working backwards, while *forward planning* is knowing the start date and working forwards. If your improved accounts receivable system must be running live on 6 April, the first day of the financial year, you would enter that as the end date and work backwards through the network to find the latest start date; but if the plan is to start development on 1 June, you would enter that as the start date and estimate the earliest date the project would be completed.

Either way, it is possible to calculate the following and place the answer in each activity node:

Start date
This is the date on which the specific activity begins and, unless the project is in the unlikely time scale of hours, it is assumed to be the daily business start time.

End date
This is the date on which the specific activity ends and is usually the end of the business day.

The critical path
By adding the total elapsed times of each of the parallel paths through the network, you can easily arrive at the one that takes longest. This is known as the critical path and is also the shortest possible time in which the project can be completed.

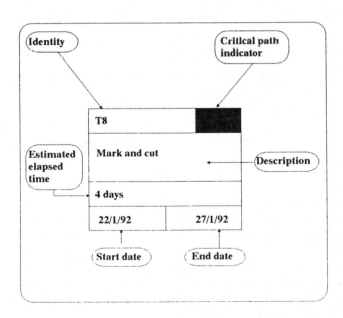

Figure 3.5 *Features of an activity node*

Non-critical paths

Of course, by identifying the critical path activities, it follows that you have automatically identified all those activities that are non-critical. These are the groups of activities which, because of the influence of other longer parallel paths, have a larger time frame for completion than the sum of the elapsed times of all that path's activities. This free time is the float time.

If you are using a computerised scheduling package, you may wonder what the long explanation about entering activity start and end dates and identifying critical and non-critical paths is all about. The reason is that these factors are identified and calculated automatically, using the project start or end dates and the elapsed times, which provides yet another good reason for using a package.

Network drawing guidelines

There are some basic guidelines which you should adhere to when developing a network diagram (refer to Figure 3.2 to help you understand this section).

Parallel groups of activities must start and end with a milestone node

This is an activity with an elapsed time of zero and is really a way of inserting an event. Following this guideline will ensure that your network diagram not only *is* a logical model of the project, it will *look* logical as well.

There must be only one start and one end node

If you find that this is not the case because the project starts simultaneously at many different points, you must create a milestone node (with an elapsed time of zero) and link it to the front of all the previously independent start nodes.

There must be no dangles

It is logical to assume that, if there is only one start and one end point, there can be no loose nodes anywhere along the network. If you create a free hanging node, known as a dangle, you should link it back into the diagram, probably at the next milestone node. In fact this is an excellent argument in favour of incorporating milestone nodes.

There can be no looping sequences of activities
It is obviously impossible to continue carrying out a sequence of activities ad infinitum. A loop is illogical because it links a later activity to an earlier one. You may wonder therefore why I mention this guideline in the first place. The reason is that it is possible to repeat a sequence once or twice and, in this case, the tendency is simply to link the sequence into a loop. Rather repeat the sequence again to ensure the diagram remains logical.

Try to ensure that the diagram flows in a single direction
This can be either from left to right or top to bottom, because it is more difficult to follow if arrows are pointing in all directions and if they are constantly crossing over each other.

The value of a network diagram
A completed network diagram is a valuable output from the planning phase because it provides you with the following features:

1. A model
It is a complete and easy-to-read model of the entire project.

2. Critical monitoring points
It can be used to identify critical stages in the project which will become sensitive monitoring points during the operational phase. These are events which, when monitored, will give an instant indication of whether the project is about to run into trouble with its constraints. Although they tend to be project specific, they could include:

- Overtime hours expected on specified activities
- A selection of milestone nodes on the critical path and their completion dates
- Dates on which to check on the arrival of critical material resources
- A definition of the quality of output required at specified points
- Critical inspection points by external inspectors
- The minimum requirements at project hand-over.

I will address these issues again in the operational phase section of the handbook.

3. Usable float time

It identifies the non-critical sections of the project that provide you with planning leeway. Those activities or groups of activities which occur on non-critical paths, and therefore have float time, can be planned to fit in at any time during their overall time scale. This means that you do not necessarily have to start these groups of activities as early as possible and leave all your float time to the end, but can spread the load of your human resources and, as a result, achieve greater productivity.

Gantt charts

Introduction

Gantt charts, named after Henry Gantt, are probably the oldest planning technique. They come in various forms, sometimes as elaborate magnetic boards, simple diagrams on graph paper, or output from a computerised scheduling tool. They are also known as bar charts.

A Gantt chart is a graphic diagram which uses all the information identified in and written into the network diagram nodes and converts it to a scaled drawing. Its strength lies in that it is drawn in graph form. The vertical axis contains a list of all the activities as far as possible in occurrence sequence, and the horizontal axis, the project time to a suitable scale. Each activity is represented by a horizontal line in its correct place in the overall time scale and the correct length according to its duration.

Figure 3.6 is a Gantt chart of part of the carpentry project described in the network diagram in Figure 3.2. Note the following:

- The horizontal scale is in days which gives a clear indication of the relative length of each activity.
- Critical path activities are the black lines, while the shaded ones represent the non-critical activities.
- Weekends when no work is done are shown as vertical shaded sections. Note that when activities T4 and T8 span a weekend the two weekend days are not included in the overall time.
- The non-critical activities T6, T7 and T12 fit within the critical activities and can be clearly seen to occupy less time than the critical activities they fall under.

If you set about drawing a Gantt chart from the information on your network diagram, you will find it an extremely laborious task. However, if you are using a computerised project scheduling package, it is usually a simple matter of pressing the right buttons.

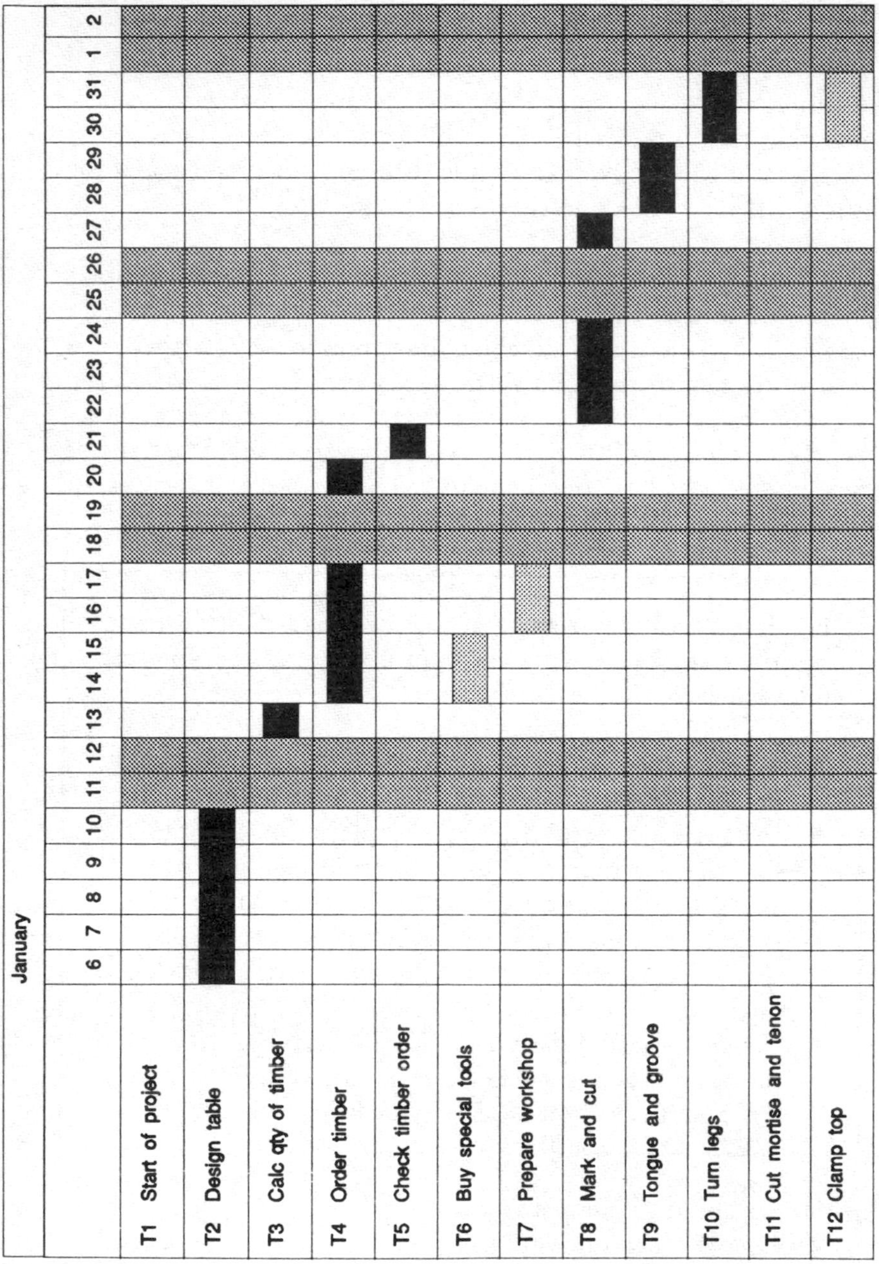

Figure 3.6   Gantt chart

If at this stage you are still developing your plan manually, please stop and think for a minute of the amount of work you could be saving yourself.

You may be asking why you should produce a Gantt chart when the network diagram already tells all. If so take a look at a Gantt chart and its corresponding network diagram and then ask yourself the question: 'Which one would I use to present my project plan to the PMB?' The answer, of course, is the Gantt chart – it is an infinitely better reporting tool.

Communication advantages
Let us look at some of the communication advantages you can expect from a Gantt chart (Figure 3.7, which is shown on page 84, gives a clear indication of the points described below).

Delayed activities
It shows any delays between one activity and the next. You could argue that, if you care to look at the start date of a successor activity on a network diagram node and compare it with the end date of its immediate predecessor, you would discover the same information. The point is that on a Gantt chart it is graphically shown – you *see* the delay. Usually an activity is delayed when it has a fixed start time (for instance, a specified delivery date for materials), with its only relationship to its predecessor being that it must not start until the predecessor is complete.

Overlapping activities
It shows that an activity can start before its immediate predecessor is complete. It often happens in a project that an activity can start as soon as *some* output from its predecessor is available. A Gantt chart will show you exactly how long the predecessor activity must be running before you are able to start its successor activity.

Float time
I have already mentioned that non-critical activities have float time. A Gantt chart shows this graphically and to scale, making it easier to see how much float is available in a group of activities and consequently making it easier to place non-critical activities

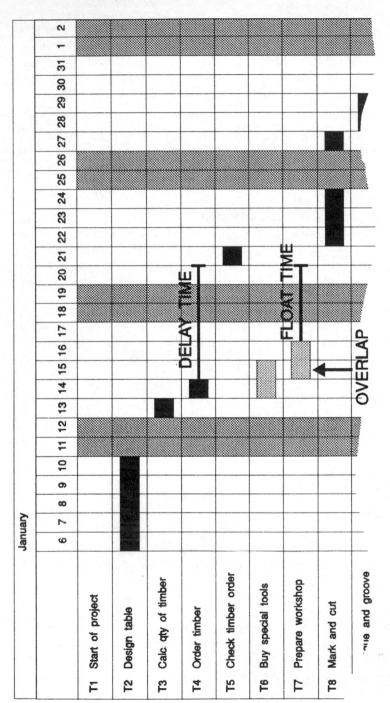

Figure 3.7   *Gantt chart showing delay, overlap and float*

within the overall plan. I shall have much more to say about float times and how to use them in the operational phase section.

Resource allocation

I have not yet discussed how you allocate specific resources, both human and material, to activities. I have reserved a separate heading a little later to do this. Sufficient to say here that it is very much easier to refer to a Gantt chart for resource allocation because you can see a model of the entire project to scale, which allows you to avoid allocating the same resource to two overlapping activities.

Reporting

I pointed out earlier that members of the PMB and any other interested parties would have a lot less trouble reading a Gantt chart than they would a network diagram. Computerised scheduling packages all have fairly dramatic ways of showing progress during the operational phase of a project, making it a simple task for you to provide regular progress report. The Gantt chart remains the same; it is just a matter of entering the completed activities and reprinting at regular intervals. I shall have more to say about this in the operational phase section.

Allocation of resources

Introduction

So far you have been shown how to develop a network diagram and how to derive a Gantt chart from it. I have also said that it takes many passes through the entire planning process before the plan is acceptable. This is referred to as refining the plan. However, to this point, you have only entered the estimated elapsed times against your known standard project activities. You are now ready, on this your first pass through the planning process, to allocate human and material resources to the project activities.

As a responsible project manager you do, of course, know your team and their capabilities and the materials available to you. In the unlikely event of your not being fully aware of the resources available to you, I suggest that you get this information immediately before proceeding any further.

Using the Gantt chart as a base, examine each activity group, decide who is to do it and what materials are needed, then allocate resources to each activity within the group. Repeat this operation for all activity groups.

This may sound extremely simple, but do not be fooled; it is a very complex task and will require many passes through the Gantt chart before you get it acceptably correct. Because of the inherent storage ability of a computer system, you will find this iterative task much easier if you are using a computerised scheduling package.

Resource allocation guidelines

I am now going to give you some guidelines to help you allocate resources effectively – many of the functions described are automatically calculated within a computer package.

Time estimates

The standard time estimates already entered are accurate as long as you are using 'standard' people to carry them out. Of course, there is no such thing as the 'standard' person because everyone has different experience and skill levels. Therefore, many of the standard elapsed times you have already entered against activities may be affected by the quality of the people carrying them out. A highly experienced team is likely to shorten time estimates while an inexperienced team may lengthen them. This in itself can become a factor when selecting resources to handle a group of activities for, if the activities are on the critical path and very time-constrained, it would be better policy to allocate an experienced team to handle them, while activities on a non-critical path could be given to a relatively inexperienced team.

There will be some activities which as yet have no elapsed times against them. How these are entered will be revealed shortly when we discuss time estimating.

Lead times

When allocating material resources, ask yourself if there is an ordering lead time. Many manufactured materials are supplied on a made-to-order basis. You must make sure that you know this so you can put an activity into the plan at the time the goods are to be ordered and not just when they are to be used. If you will be using equipment to develop the project (such as a computer to develop a computer system) you may want to find out the availability and any constraints that may be applied.

Cost estimates

People are employed on a rate per time period basis. You must know the rate for each team member so you can apply it to the elapsed time to give a total cost for the activity. Carrying out this exercise may change some of the allocations simply for economic reasons. I have discussed using experienced and inexperienced teams. It is a fact that one pays more for experience; therefore, it may be better to give a long, non-critical group of activities to an inexperienced and less costly team for a better economic result.

Similarly, you must find out the terms under which material resources are to be made available. You may be buying the materials outright, leasing them, hiring them or paying for them on a time-used basis. If you have a payment choice with a specific piece of equipment, choose the one that provides the best economic arrangement.

Many costing operations will be part of your organisation's standard practices, so I suggest you are aware of these before spending too much time working out great economic savings.

> **If at this stage you are starting to think that allocating resources is a bit of a juggling act, you are starting to grasp the complexities of the operation.**

Percentage of time used

Just in case you thought you had resource allocation completely under control, let me introduce another complexity. Some activities are known to take a specified time to complete. However, those carrying them out may not be required to be fully committed. Perhaps, in some cases, only half their time is needed to complete the activity within the time scale. This obviously affects your cost estimates because you can hardly charge team members at their full rates if they are only partly committed. A bit of arithmetic is needed to ensure that the correct cost estimates are calculated.

Reducing time estimates

Before even considering reducing the estimated elapsed time of the project, consider this axiom:

> **Generally a reduction in the estimated elapsed project time results in a corresponding increase in project cost.**

If, after allocating resources and times to a group of activities, you find that the time taken is going to be unacceptably long, you can shorten it in a number of ways:

Change the human resources
I have already discussed the use of more experienced team members to shorten the duration of an activity so this is only a reminder.

Increase the human resources
This is based on the assumption that, if you put more people on to an activity, it will take less time to do. This is generally true, but remember that you increase the administration and the cost, not only by adding the rate of the extra people used, but also through the reduction in productivity as well, because doubling the number of people does not automatically halve the elapsed time.

To help you understand resource increase complexities, consider a project which requires a hole a half metre square by three metres deep to be dug. If one person could dig the hole at a rate of two hours per metre, the entire project would take six hours. However, if you allocated two people to dig the hole you could presumably get it done in three hours.

Wrong! Two people could not fit into the hole at the same time, therefore the correct estimate is still six hours.

Wrong again! When you calculated the time for one worker to dig the hole you included rest time. This must now be taken off because rest time could be taken while the other person was digging. However, because someone is now required to control the project to ensure that the workers get adequate rest, you have increased the administration load and the cost.

Upgrade the material resources
This is an excellent way to improve productivity on the basis that better equipment means better throughput. Remember, though, that you are more than likely going to increase the cost. There is an old saying in the computer industry, 'If it takes too long to process, throw more hardware at it!' This works, but you often end up generating a host of software costs to support the hardware upgrade which, in their turn, slow down the new equipment, resulting in a similar throughput at a greater cost.

Downgrade the quality
This is a difficult one because it involves you going back to the

PMB and telling them that, in order to complete the project in time, you are going to provide them with inferior output. Of course, if the PMB can live with that, you have established a good way of reducing the elapsed time.

Phase the completion
Once again this involves tricky discussion with the PMB. It may be agreeable to your providing the output over a period of time instead of all at once.

Resource usage histograms

There is a tool which you can use to give a graphic display of resource usage called a resource usage histogram, see Figure 3.8.

It is a graph with the vertical axis representing resource usage by time period, and the horizontal axis representing time. The result for each resource is a series of connected blocks showing the usage of resources related to a specific time period.

I do not recommend that you draw histograms manually; rather rely on your computerised scheduling package which will almost certainly produce them by combining input to your Gantt chart and your actual resource allocation details. An added advantage is that the horizontal axis (ie the time) is shown at the same scale as that on the Gantt chart, allowing for very simple comparison.

Resource usage histograms have a number of uses:

Identifying over-allocation of resources
By simply drawing a horizontal line at a point above which you consider a resource to be over-used, you can easily identify this potential problem.

Showing resource availability
A histogram allows you to show the individual resource commitment across an entire project. This allows you to see at a glance whether a resource is totally committed or available, thus allowing you to allocate leave at a convenient time, or to reallocate the resource to another activity.

Collective resource usage
By combining resources performing a similar task, you can see when specific members of your team are fully used or available.

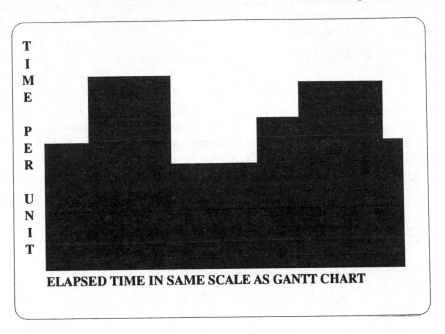

Figure 3.8 *Resource usage histogram*

Resource levelling
By examining both individual and collective histograms, you can smooth the usage of resources so that, rather than a series of peaks and troughs, you have a relatively constant commitment. You will probably never achieve a completely smooth profile on your histograms so do not try; your commitment should be to achieve one that is acceptably smooth.

A reporting tool
A resource usage histogram provides a graphic and meaningful reporting link between you and your team, and often goes a long way towards managing requests for intermittent time off.

Time estimates

Introduction

In this section we shall consider the process of estimating time. Remember, however, that whenever a time is put on an activity and a resource is allocated to that activity, the cost can then be calculated. Costs are therefore not considered as estimates, but rather as accurate calculations based on the time multiplied by the unit cost of the resource. The fact that the time estimate may be inaccurate is something you must always bear in mind when calculating costs.

Because this is a handbook, I am able to indulge in the luxury of compartmentalising the planning process under different headings. You do not have this luxury. I have stated more than once that you will be carrying out all the planning operations in an iterative cycle, completing more and more each time until the plan is acceptably complete. Time estimation is part of the iterative process.

There are many techniques for estimating times accurately and there have been far more books printed and courses conducted on the subject. It is a vital part of planning because:

- It is from the time estimates that costs are calculated.
- It establishes the contractual end date of the project.
- The success of the operational phase rests on the accuracy of the time estimates made during planning.

With this in mind I would like to make this statement:

You cannot consider yourself a competent project manager until you know that you can estimate times accurately.

Estimating guidelines

Let us look at estimating and see what you can do to become good at it:

Get personal experience

We all know that the best way to be good at estimating the time for an activity accurately is to have done it before. Say, for instance, that it takes you six hours to drive from point A to point B. You know this because you have done the trip many times in the same car. So when asked, 'What time can we expect you?', you can answer, 'At 12 noon', accurately because you know you are leaving at 6 a.m.

Experience comes with time; therefore it is a hopelessly inaccurate estimating method if you are an inexperienced project manager.

Use other people's experience

If you do not have the experience, someone else is bound to have it, so it is simply a matter of approaching the correct person and making your request. I have stated that as simply as possible so you can see how easy it is. The unbelievable fact is that people do *not* ask others enough, relying rather on their own intuition, probably through one of the most irritating of human failings, the fear of appearing stupid or losing face – known as ego defence.

If you have allocated a particular activity to someone in your team, you have presumably done so because that person has experience of the activity. So go to that person and ask how long it will take to complete. This has the double benefit of getting an accurate time estimate from someone with experience and motivating your team member into a commitment to achieve it.

Use documented experience

Experience is often recorded. It is only for you to know where to find it and look it up. Let us return to our point A to point B analogy. The first time you do the trip, you do not know how long it will take you, so you consult the road map and find out that someone has very kindly provided a distance/time chart. You are therefore able to obtain a standard time which you can adjust according to the car you are driving and the speed at which you generally like to travel.

Document your own experience

On the premise that documented experience is only available

because someone took the trouble to write it down, document your own. This you can selfishly do privately so that you become the most indispensable project manager in your organisation, or you can do it in a form that everyone can access.

This is a good time to bring up the subject of standards. All organisations have standards manuals to help inexperienced staff learn their requirements and generally to ensure that everyone in the organisation is doing the job a similar way to a specified quality. Why not ensure that standard time estimates for projects form a section of your standards manual? And who better to get this ball rolling than you, the project manager!

To a certain extent, using a computerised scheduling package ensures that your time estimates are recorded in an accessible way for future projects. Unfortunately, they are kept in project sequence. How nice it would be if all estimates could be extracted from the projects once complete and stored together in an estimating dictionary with similar activities grouped together. One or two software suppliers have thought of this and have developed or are developing systems that link to their computerised scheduling packages and carry out the process described.

Use an estimating technique

There are documented established estimating techniques available which you can use. It requires prior investigation to select a method which must then become a standard in your organisation. I stress this because it is no good your knowing and using a method and the rest of the team using some other method or none at all, probably resulting in inaccurate time estimates.

A popular method, which was initially developed for sizing computer software systems, is known as Function Point Analysis (FPA) in which standard factors are applied to various activity types, reducing them all to a common denominator known as a function point count. I stress again that for this method to be successful it must be implemented throughout your organisation and a specific person appointed to control it.

Refining the model

Introduction

The model once complete must be refined to decrease the time scale, decrease the cost or improve the quality. Ways of doing this have been discussed in each of the preceding sections on logic definition. Here I present the concept of a questioning method which is outlined in Keith Lockyer's excellent book, *Critical Path Analysis and Other Project Network Techniques* (Pitman). The questions are asked as follows (I have added in one or two of my own):

Examine the purpose of the project:
What is being done?
Why is it being done?
What else could be done?
What should be done?
Could it be done any better?

Examine the project environment:
Where is it being done?
Why there?
Where else could it be done?
Where should it be done?
Would it be done any better elsewhere?

Examine the sequence of activities:
When are they being done?
Why then?
When else could they be done?
When should they be done?
Would changing their sequence improve the end result?

Examine the human resources:
Who is doing it?
Why that person?
Who else might do it?
Who should do it?
Would someone else do it better?

Examine the method being used:
    How is it being done?
    Why that way?
    How else can it be done?
    Could the way it is being done be improved?

The process

As the iterative nature of plan development has often been mentioned, I do not need to labour the point here. It is a good time to summarise the steps in the planning cycle:

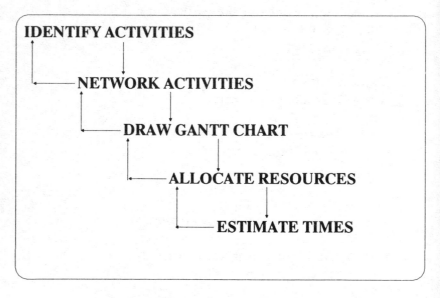

Figure 3.9 *The iterative nature of the planning cycle*

Identify the activities

Use standard activity lists and modify them according to the specific requirements of this project. Sequence is not important nor is it a problem if some information is unavailable.

Network the activities

Use a computerised project scheduling tool to enter the activities, arrange them into logical groups, and sequence them both serially and in parallel in a network diagram. Insert elapsed times where known.

Draw a Gantt chart

This is an automatic result of the networking process, but in a much more readable format. Use it as a basis for further development of the plan and as a progress reporting tool.

Allocate the resources

Examine each activity in the Gantt chart and allocate people and materials to it. Juggle until you arrive at an acceptable solution.

Estimate the times

Use a combination of the methods described. Be absolutely certain that every time estimate is accurate to the best of your ability. Do not guess.

Repeat the process until acceptable

Refine the plan by repeating the steps over and over again. Talk to interested parties about it. Make certain that your plan is not only acceptable to you, but that others think it will work as well.

Introduction

The project schedule

The presentation

Do not just hand over the plan for approval; do a proper presentation to explain contents and invite questions

This is an explanatory and contractual document which contains:

A synopsis of the project

Functional project maps

NCS project maps

Network diagrams at every level of the project

A list of the critical monitoring points

Gantt charts

Resource usage histograms for human and material resources

Financial reports of overall cost broken down by sub-project with cash flows

Explanations where necessary of how activities will be done

The contract itself ready for signing

Agreement is required before proceeding with the operational phase

Constant communication throughout the planning process will ensure that this part of the process goes smoothly

Planning output

Introduction

You have completed your plan, but you have not done this in splendid isolation. At every step in the process you have sought advice, agreed various procedures, requested changes, and kept team members informed of their coming role. Remember that, as the project manager, you are the great communicator; you do not plan a project behind closed doors. In fact, it is a tribute to your skill as a project manager when you carry out the presentation of your plan to a PMB that already understands and has contributed to much of the work that has gone into it.

Now is the time to prepare your output so that the final and contractual agreement can be obtained to proceed with the operational phase.

The project schedule

You must prepare a document known as the project schedule. The document will contain everything you have already produced during the logic definition stage but remember to include:

A synopsis

To show in a concise document why the project was conceived, what it is going to do, when it will be complete, where it is going to be carried out, how it is going to be done, who is going to do it.

The synopsis also provides an introduction to the other documents and an easy reference to finding and interpreting them.

Functional project maps

The completed maps showing all the contractors and sub-contractors involved in the development of the project provide an extremely clear and concise guide to the project members.

NCS project maps

This is also a clear and concise document which provides invaluable information about what you are going to do, why you are going to do it, and when you are going to do it.

Network diagrams

These show the sequence of activities both serially and in parallel and the overall duration of the project.

Critical monitoring points

Include your list of critical monitoring points and what action you intend taking if any of them fail to be met, so that the PMB knows exactly how you intend to control the project and provide early warning of potential problems.

Gantt charts

These provide clear graphic pictures of the activities and when they occur and shows what the progress reports are going to look like.

Resource usage histograms

These show the commitment of resources to the project.

Financial reports
These show how much the project is going to cost both overall, in stages, and for individual material and human resources, and to give the PMB an accurate view of the required cash flow.

Activity explanations
These show in typewritten form full details if necessary of how you intend to carry out activity groups and individual activities within them.

The contract
This is a covering document which, when signed by you and the PMB, becomes the legal binding contract for the project.

The presentation

A project plan should never simply be given to the PMB for signature. It should be presented – and by that I do not mean handing it over with a respectful little bow. A presentation is a well-planned delivery done in front of the PMB which explains the content of the project schedule and invites questions. Only after the presentation, which may in itself require you to carry out some minor alterations to the plan, do you hand it over for signature. Here are some tips towards providing an interesting presentation:

Prepare carefully
Make sure that you know what you are going to say and how you are going to say it. Use simple but effective tools, such as overhead transparencies and a white board or a flip chart, to help you through your presentation and to underline some of the important points raised.

Prepare the presentation environment
Make sure that the room is available, that the overhead projector is there and working, that there are pens for the white board, and that the seating is adequate for the attendees. Make sure that you are dressed neatly.

The presentation

Stand tall and deliver your presentation with confidence. Use body and hand movements; do not stand in one place looking like an erect corpse. Ask questions where necessary and allow an adequate time for answers – and listen to the answers. At the end summarise your presentation, give definite time limits on the feedback you will give to unanswered questions, leave a copy of the project plan with instructions that it is read through and that any unclear points are raised within a given time scale.

You have a plan acceptable to both you and the PMB. You are now completely prepared to enter the operational phase of the project.

Introduction   Inception phase   Planning phase   Operational phase

Introduction
Monitoring
Reporting
Variations
Quality
Hand-over
Review

Introduction

There are many things that can put a project off-track; at least ensure that it starts smoothly and on time

While you cannot motivate staff, you can provide a climate in which motivation can take place

Monitoring

Use the critical monitoring points

Monitor on a digital rather than an analogue basis

Monitor staff for:
Reduction in commitment
Decrease in motivation
Deteriorating inter-personal relations
Disruptive members

Progress reporting

Report according to policy

Reports include:
Written assessment
Gantt charts with updated progress
Cash used to date against plan
Variations from plan

Variations & replanning

Do not ignore warning signals

Variations from:
Technology change
Financial change
Change in sponsor
Downgrading

Report contains:
Source
How identified
Exact nature
Problem analysis
Additional costs
Recommended solutions

Quality assurance

Quality must be agreed and quantified before starting

External inspection points

Hand-over

Final quality checks
Testing
External inspection
Signing off
Rework of minor finishing problems
File the project documents

Critical review

Overview of project
Reporting quality
Meeting constraints
Variations
Rework

4. *The Operational Phase*

Introduction

The operational phase, like the planning phase, is under your control. Just as you were responsible for producing an acceptable working plan, you are now responsible and accountable for the implementation of the project.

This is the time when all your leadership skills are required, for you must not only control the administration aspects but also ensure that your team remains motivated throughout the project. We shall discuss motivation a little later, but for the moment ponder on this:

> **Motivating people is only possible if you create a climate in which motivation can take place.**

Your first task is to activate the project. During the planning phase, contractual arrangements were made between you and the PMB, between you and sub-contractors, and even between sub-contractors and other sub-contractors. By referring to the project schedule output from the planning phase, you know the start dates of every sub-contractor who reports to you. Now you must make certain that everyone starts their group of activities at the correct time.

> **There is nothing more soul destroying than a project starting late, because it immediately puts you into catch-up mode, and into a situation from which you will probably never recover.**

There may be many things you have to do to activate part of the (or the whole) project. These include making sure the human resources are assembled and ready to start work, making sure the material resources are available and ready for use, and ensuring that the planned financial arrangements are made. The activation of the project is so important I am going to repeat the axiom just stated in a slightly different way:

> **Remember, so many things can happen during the operational phase that can put the project off-track – at least ensure that it starts off smoothly.**

During the operational phase you will constantly be referring to the project schedule, for in that document lie all the details of your agreed and achievable plan. However, if you have used a computer package to prepare the schedule, you will often be sitting in front of the computer updating progress.

There are many things that will need your attention from this point until the end of the project:

- You must obviously monitor progress.
- You must provide reports to all parties so that everyone is aware of the progress being made.
- You must become aware of variations in the planned operation so that you can immediately go into replanning mode.
- You must monitor the quality of output.

- You must be there at hand-over time to ensure that the project owner finds the output acceptable.
- You must be prepared to carry out a critical project review when it is all over.

Throughout this time you must exercise your leadership skills, making sure that project members are motivated, solving conflicts, arranging personnel adjustments where necessary, and generally keeping yourself fully informed throughout.

The sections which follow deal with all these aspects.

Monitoring

A project is *not* easy to monitor. It may have seemed that it was going to be so as a result of the carefully produced plan, but there are myriad items to consider, most of which could derail the project.

We discussed the identification of critical monitoring points during the planning phase and I said that we would return to the subject in the operational phase. Well, now is the time to revisit that section and see how you are going to use critical monitoring points to assist in keeping the project on track.

If you remember I told you to develop a list of events which, when monitored, would give you an instant indication of whether the project is about to run into trouble with its constraints. Typical events stated were:

- Overtime hours expected on specified activities
- A selection of milestone nodes on the critical path and their completion dates
- Material arrival dates
- A definition of the quality of output expected at specified points
- Critical inspection points by outside inspectors
- The minimum requirements at project hand-over time.

> **A list of critical monitoring points enables you to check the project's progress on a digital rather than an analogue basis.**

By this I mean that you do not monitor project progress by holding a regular Monday morning meeting to discover that something went wrong the previous Tuesday, and is now too far gone to put right; rather you find out about potential problem areas *before* or, at worst, *just as* they happen.

Of course, the success of this method depends on the careful selection of the critical monitoring points. This is not as difficult as you might imagine because:

- Many of them will become apparent by virtue of being important milestones in the project.
- Some are a result of outside inspection and are required by law or, in the case of in-house projects, by the internal audit department.
- Your network diagram accurately reflects lead times for materials so you have important dates readily to hand.

Other critical monitoring points are often project specific and become apparent during planning.

However, it is not enough simply to monitor in the way I have described; you are also a manager of people who must be motivated to produce the required output in the specified time. You must be immediately sensitive to the following:

- Any reduction in the commitment of key personnel
- A general decrease in staff motivation levels
- A deterioration in interpersonal relationships
- A member of the staff who is acting in a disruptive manner.

While it is relatively simple to identify a problem with a material resource and repair it, people are much more complex because you are not aware of *when* they go wrong and it is much more difficult to find out exactly *what* is wrong.

Providing constantly good leadership is extremely difficult. In the planning phase we said that some of the functions of your daily work schedule are to lead, organise and control. Practise and improve your leadership qualities constantly at work, and ensure that you attend a course that deals with these complex and important issues.

You've no doubt heard the expression, 'Different strokes for different folks.' Remember that not everyone is motivated by the same things. You must provide a climate in which motivation can take place and this involves knowing what drives your staff to work better.

Typical motivational triggers are:

Money. This cannot be ignored as being unimportant, because otherwise I could ask, why on earth are we all working in the first place? Remember that, although money motivates people to work, it does not necessarily provide a constant impetus. Salespeople, through commission payments, are more motivated to work for money but most project team members are required to work for just their own salary.

Enthusiasm. If you are genuinely enthusiastic about the project this is bound to rub off on your staff. Enthusiasm is infectious so, if you feel it, make sure everyone knows about it.

Clear objectives. One of the most important parts of the planning phase was to develop a clear idea of what everyone on the project had to do, when they had to do it, and why it had to be done. People like to have clear objectives; make sure that these are not muddied during the course of the project.

Job satisfaction. People like to know they are working on a job that provides them with a degree of satisfaction. No one likes to work continuously on repetitive boring tasks. Make sure that you allocate the work so that everyone is able to achieve a degree of job satisfaction.

Creativity. This is a difficult one, for the very nature of a clear project plan is one which has no room for interpretation. It is hard to be creative when you are locked into a narrow, clearly defined route. Perhaps allowing staff members to become involved in tricky parts of the planning process will allow for creativity. I ask only that you remember it is the trigger that gets many people going.

Well-established methods. Just to show you that there are opposites, some people are motivated by the fact that the method is an established, well-proven one, and shy away from creativity of any sort.

Positive reinforcement. Many people require some positive statement from their manager when they feel they have done a good job. Do not be patronising about it but, whenever you can, hand out positive reinforcement for a job well done.

Status. This is important to many people and can take different forms. People like a clearly defined work area, their own office, responsibility and authority. Within the framework of company policy and the project itself, ensure that your team's ego is adequately fed.

Reporting on progress

During the planning phase you agreed the reporting structure as well as the nature of the reports themselves. The value of this decision now becomes apparent for, if the system was not already in place and you *now* decide how to keep people informed, you would probably have disagreement, confusion, and ultimately conflict which would be extremely difficult to resolve, given the time constraints imposed during the operational phase.

All computerised project scheduling packages have methods for monitoring and reporting on progress and, if your project had been planned with the aid of such a package, you would have agreed the reporting structure which was incorporated.

At the highest level, the progress reports go from you directly to the PMB. However, in order to produce your reports, you require similar reports from the sub-contractors reporting to you, and they in turn from their sub-contractors, and so on to the lowest level in the hierarchy. It is absolutely vital that all project members are made aware of their reporting responsibilities because, as you will no doubt have gathered, if someone fails to report, the entire system is in danger of breaking down. As project manager, it is your responsibility to ensure that the system works and remains working throughout the operational phase.

Reports should include:

- A written, backed up by a verbal, assessment of progress
- Gantt charts updated to show progress to date against the plan
- Reports of financial commitment to date against plan. This is an extremely useful report for monitoring over- or under-expenditure
- Reports on variations on the agreed critical monitoring points. I will have more to say about variations in the section which follows.

Variations and replanning

As the old saying goes, 'The best laid plans of mice and men . . .' It is no good blissfully sitting back after producing your magnificent plan and assuming that the operational phase will happen without a hitch. We would all like this to be the case and, believe it or not, sometimes it actually does happen.

> **It is an extremely unwise project manager who ignores warning signals of potential problems during the operational phases of a project.**

A problem only becomes a variation when it cannot be solved without affecting the time, money and quality constraints imposed on the project. You and each sub-contractor have signed a contract which clearly spelt out these constraints; it is only when they must be altered at whatever level of the project hierarchy they occur that they must be reported as variations to the next level.

If the problem can be overcome at the higher hierarchical level, it need go no further. It follows, therefore, that many variations can occur during the operational phase of a project without the PMB ever hearing about them. This method of reporting variations and solving problems is very effective and results in minimal panic situations.

How does a variation happen? Well, they are a result of interference from three areas.

External factors

These occur when the PMB itself decides on a change for reasons outside of the project.

These could include:

- A change in technology
- Loss of financial backing
- A new project sponsor with new ideas
- Downgrading to bring the project back on to budget
- A change in product development
- A change in legislation.

Any of these examples and other external events could result at worst in the cancellation of the project and at best in the development of an updated plan.

Internal factors

These happen as a result of a variation report. This is a good time to outline the contents of a variation report. It should contain:

- The source of the variation
- How it was identified
- The exact nature of the variation
- An analysis of the resulting problem if it is not corrected
- Additional costs and time that will be incurred
- Recommended solutions.

Micro planning

During the operational phase, many plans that earlier could only be known in a macro sense must be converted to micro plans. This can result in time and therefore financial estimates having to be altered. If macro plans developed during the planning phase are estimated pessimistically rather than optimistically, most variations occurring through micro planning will be avoided.

Obviously, a variation report will result in a certain amount of replanning. It is important that you do not regard this exercise as any different from the actual planning phase of the project. Replanning is, in fact, a project in its own right, so use all the discipline that you used when planning and make absolutely certain that everyone affected by the changed plan is kept informed.

Quality assurance

Unless the exact nature of the quality expected has been clearly established during the planning phase, you have put yourself in line for many arguments and unresolved conflicts. This once again highlights the importance of establishing *all* the facts and writing them into the contract at the planning phase.

> **It is no good arguing about unacceptable quality of output when you never agreed what that quality should be in the first place.**

As with variations and replanning, quality assurance can be controlled from inside or outside the project.

External control

In a high risk development the results of which are going to be used by members of the public, there are standard external inspection points required by law. These would obviously be known to you and would have been identified as activities during the planning phase. If the output is rejected during an external inspection, you must complete a variation report and plan for a re-inspection activity once the problem is rectified.

Internal control

The quality of the output was agreed during the planning phase and, as part of your monitoring responsibility, you must ensure that quality standards remain acceptable. Agreeing a quality standard brings up the point of measurement. Do not simply agree that the output must be of an 'acceptable quality' whatever you may mean; spell out in clear terms a quantified standard. In the case of an improved accounts receivable system, this may be difficult to do, but it is by no means impossible. Simply think of what the end user wants from the system and turn those wants into quantifiable quality assessments.

Hand-over

When you outlined the reporting policy in the planning phase, you defined the hand-over procedures. These would include:

- Final quality checks
- Testing the finished product
- External inspection
- The signing-off procedure.

Quite often at this stage, probably because the project manager is not totally happy with the final output, many projects move from the operational phase to become an end product without any proper sign off. It is important, however, that this is done both to be able to ensure that the final output is in fact as specified, and to have a point at which the project is declared complete.

Although the output from the project may be accepted as workable, sometimes there are minor alterations that must be done before the PMB registers its total approval. In this case you must ensure that referrals for rework are agreed and completed and that in effect a contract to carry out the minor finishing tasks is drawn up.

This in itself produces a number of problems, the most common being that:

- Motivation levels to complete the work are low and need a great deal of reinforcing.
- The end product is actually being used, thus complicating the work.
- The project team could easily be involved in a new project and not have the time.

As long as you treat the rework as a project in its own right, you should be able to obviate most of the completion problems.

Once the project is totally complete including any rework, the only thing that remains is for you to file the project documents and report that it is complete.

Critical review

In order to ensure that you always improve your handling of future projects, it is important that you and the project members take part in a formal critical project review.

It could be argued that, if you had developed the project according to the guidelines described in this handbook, you would not need to carry out a review because you would have been monitoring, reporting on and solving problems as they occurred throughout the project. While this is true, those problems occurred in the heat of the moment and were solved at the time they occurred in isolation from one another. A project review allows you to look *objectively* at the entire project and develop strategies to ensure that problems have adequate solutions should they occur again.

An independent person, preferably outside the project, should chair the project review meeting. You must of course attend, and make sure that representatives from the PMB are present as well as senior members of your project team. Let us examine the points to be covered:

An overview of the entire project. This should be as seen by you, the PMB and your team. Each group should be allowed to offer comment which is then discussed. Use the NCS project map and go through it carefully to see that all necessary conditions for success were met.

The quality of the reporting. If any feelings are expressed reflecting on the quality of the reporting, a discussion must take place immediately to ensure that this is improved in the next project.

The time, money and quality constraints. If any of these factors do not agree with the plan, they must be discussed and the reasons established. It's no good saying, 'Oh, well, we overshot budget again,' because that will never cure the problem. You must investigate and find out why it went wrong and make sure you will do better next time.

Variation reports. If any variations have been generated during the project, these should be looked at to see what caused them. Doing this often results in improved quality in future projects, for it is in the area of poor quality that most projects are held up. Maybe the meeting will identify sloppy work by specific team members who can then be questioned on the poor performance or, better still, given guidance and training to handle the work better next time.

Any rework. If the project has been handed over but there is a requirement to rework some of the output because of inferior quality then, as you did with the variation reports, identify the responsible people.

Make sure that the meeting is minuted so that the review report can be distributed, ideas arising incorporated in your standards manual for future projects, and finally filed with the project documents.

Never go to a meeting without this handbook. It will be invaluable as a prompt to ensure that you always ask all the right questions.

Further Reading from Kogan Page

Andersen, E, Grude, K, Haug, T and Turner, J (1989) *Goal Directed Project Management*

Burton, C and Michael, N (1992) *A Practical Guide to Project Management*

Davies, M (1992) *Project Management* (Workshop Package)

Haynes, M (1990) *Project Management: From Idea to Implementation*

A full list of titles on management and business is available from the publisher, Kogan Page Limited, 120 Pentonville Road, London N1 9JN; 071-278 0433 (phone); 071-837 6348 (fax).